T0147164

This!...is Where Love Grows

My Triumph Over Anorexia

BRENDA KYTZ BURGHARDT SHEETS

BALBOA.
PRESS

A DIVISION OF HAY HOUSE

Balboa Press books may be ordered through booksellers or by contacting:

Balboa Press
A Division of Hay House
1663 Liberty Drive
Bloomington, IN 47403
www.balboapress.com
1 (877) 407-4847

Because of the dynamic nature of the Internet, any web addresses or
links contained in this book may have changed since publication and
may no longer be valid. The views expressed in this work are solely those
of the author and do not necessarily reflect the views of the publisher,
and the publisher hereby disclaims any responsibility for them.

The author of this book does not dispense medical advice or prescribe the use
of any technique as a form of treatment for physical, emotional, or medical
problems without the advice of a physician, either directly or indirectly. The
intent of the author is only to offer information of a general nature to help
you in your quest for emotional and spiritual well-being. In the event you use
any of the information in this book for yourself, which is your constitutional
right, the author and the publisher assume no responsibility for your actions.

Any people depicted in stock imagery provided by Thinkstock are
models, and such images are being used for illustrative purposes only.
Certain stock imagery © Thinkstock.

Print information available on the last page.

ISBN: 978-1-5043-5564-3 (sc)
ISBN: 978-1-5043-5565-0 (e)

Library of Congress Control Number: 2016906080

Balboa Press rev. date: 05/26/2016

This!...is dedicated to my Mom, Jane Burghardt, whom I respect, treasure and love immensely. Thank you from the depths of my soul. You are my butterfly... flitting into my life when I needed you, but knowing when to fly away when I had to experience the world on my own. In turn, with your prayers, strong conviction and constant love you encouraged my metamorphosis from a seemingly lifeless cocoon to a vibrant and beautiful creation of God.

Praise for
This!...is Where Love Grows

"This!...is Where Love Grows" takes the reader on an emotional journey through Brenda's descent into the darkness of anorexia and her hard fought rise to recovery. Bearing all, she tells her story without sparing any brutal or raw truths of the hellish reality of day to day life as a sufferer. We are offered a rare glimpse of what it would be like to battle the demon of anorexia and the affect it has not only on the sufferer but on all those who walk this journey alongside. "This!...is Where Love Grows" offers insight and hope for those who have been touched by this disease and will resonate with both sufferers and their loved ones alike. Brenda's words give voice to those who may not yet be able to speak about their own battle with anorexia while providing their loved ones a better understanding of the disease. This book is a gift for any family that is currently dealing with, or has experienced, an eating disorder.

Carolyn Melsness
BScN

"This!...is Where Love Grows" is a courageous, vulnerable rendering of hope and healing on an emotional, physical and spiritual level. I only wish I could have read this in 1996 when my own sister was suffering from this often misunderstood disease. This is a book that will support

so many touched by anorexia and provide hope for individuals and families, especially at a time when they feel powerless.

Barbara Burke
Supervising Teacher Hoffman Institute Canada
Author of I Am Divine

"This!...is Where Love Grows" is a powerful book about a woman's journey through anorexia and how she came out on the other side alive to tell about it. I absolutely LOVED it! Her ability to be vulnerable and courageous at the same time is a powerful testimony to how she is using this experience to help both the sufferer and families through this debilitating disease. She is the true definition of a hero, a woman who, in the face of danger, combats adversity through impressive feats of ingenuity, bravery and strength, often sacrificing her own personal concerns for the greater good of humanity. In this book she bares her soul so that others can get the gift of hope and recovery. This quote summarizes her book beautifully... "You are stronger than you believe, braver than you seem and smarter than you think." ~ A.A Milne

Nik Gardiner - Life Coach
www.thechangemaker.ca

Brenda has written a compelling, vulnerable and authentic account of her experience of being close to death with anorexia. Her story of pain and recovery reveals the power of self-love, compassion and forgiveness. The reader cannot help but be inspired by what is possible for healing and transformation. "This!...is Where Love Grows" is a must read for anyone who is currently suffering with, or has ever suffered from, an eating disorder. Brenda shares how our need for unconditional love as children — and how we receive this love from our family system — shapes our beliefs, thoughts and feelings about ourselves. Her powerful journey reveals how to go beyond death and survival to actually thrive in life.

Helen Valleau, LSP
Visioning Coach
Author of *"A Year of Possibilities"* and *"100 Minutes of Inspiration"*

Brenda's sharing of her story through Canadian Mental Health Association – Calgary Region's YouthSMART program carries an important message about many aspects of mental health. Eventually successfully navigating through her own complex journey of an eating disorder gives Brenda's story the personal appeal which connects with everyone. This is especially important with youth who hear things in these presentations which might be a critical impetus for their own road to recovery.

V Joy Pavelich
Communications & Community Engagement Leader
CMHA - Calgary Region

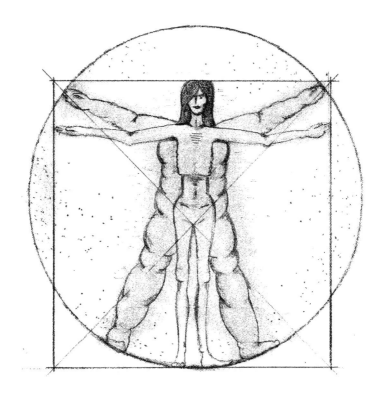

This!

...is a picture I drew, based on Leonardo da Vinci's 'Vetruvian Man'; which for me, tragically emphasizes the dichotomy of reality versus the skewed self perception in the eyes of the sufferer

"...Know I have a plan for you; a plan for hope and glory..."

Jeremiah 29:11

This...is for *YOU*, the *sufferer*

I wish to share with you a story… my story. I sit here writing to you as the survivor of a tragic disease - one that depletes not only the physical body, but also imprisons the mind and cripples the spirit. There are many causes of eating disorders and everyone's story is different. This is <u>my</u> story and I relate it <u>from my point of view</u> – that of the sufferer, the <u>survivor</u>. I do not attempt to analyze nor predict anyone else's journey. I only wish to share with those that suffer that I know – I truly know – what it is to experience the debilitating and seemingly hopeless affliction of anorexia nervosa.

Throughout my story I refer to the darkness inside me, that which negatively controlled all my thoughts and actions, as 'DEMON.' In no way do I wish to infer that I was possessed by the devil or any such thing. I just want to emphasize that there tragically exists within the sufferer of anorexia a darkness from which there is no escape…something that feels very tangible, and although I was often aware of the poor choices and hurtful decisions I was making, I truly had no control over it.

Throughout my dark time – the weeks, months, and years that I lived with the demon that inhabited my soul and who was determined to destroy me spiritually, emotionally and physically – I felt that there was a chasm between the professional that treated me and the road I stumbled along. The professionals had their 'book smarts' – the psychological and medical knowledge of how to treat the disease – but they had not 'walked the walk' of the sufferer and had no firsthand knowledge of the fear and destitution of living with the Anorexia Demon. My psychiatrist could tell me that I needed to eat in order for my mind to release its hold on me, but he could not truly understand the figurative twelve foot thick concrete wall I had to claw through in order to lift the fork to my mouth. He had no idea of the debilitating messages DEMON constantly whispered in my ear. Nor did he feel the constricting clutch of DEMON'S talons on my soul nor the twisting and churning of the black mass of self-loathing that existed inside of me.

There was no-one to truly understand me other than the fellow sufferers I met through 'support groups.' But the misguided 'support' we offered each other only added to the competition and the quest for perfection. For the relationship we shared as co-sufferers was based on comparisons of whom was stronger and more determined, who was the skinniest and winning 'the game.'

"Believe that life is worth living, and your
belief will help create the fact."
William James

Through the sharing of my story, I strive to be that connection between the professional experts and you, the sufferer. I want to be the arms that hold you and the voice that comforts you when you feel you are all alone in your despair. I want you to know that I once walked your walk and have lived your anguish and hopelessness.

I was blessed to have made it through to the other side of anorexia despite all the medical evidence saying that I should not have survived. And you too can survive, there is hope for your recovery. I am that example of hope for you. There is a spark of light within you that wants to succeed and wants to live. You <u>can</u> recover...aim for that tendril of love and hope that dangles as though it is just out of your reach. You are precious and you deserve healing. Never, ever give up...

This...is the prologue

Anorexia Nervosa affects both the sufferer and those around them. Anyone touched by its vicious claws has their lives irrevocably scarred. It affects the person and all their relationships. A very few fortunate sufferers can look back on their years of hell triumphantly, knowing they have truly and successfully battled their demons. Most, however, suffer in shame and silence for the rest of their lives – some for untold years, and others for only a few, until their bodies are literally starved and one or more organs give out – or they take their own lives surrendering to the unbearable anguish.

From the moment of birth every person's deepest desire is unconditional love and acceptance of their true essence. All personal struggles manifest from this elemental core. To fulfill this need a child may choose to either mimic or reject their parents' actions and/or beliefs, at times alternating between the dichotomies in desperation. From my earliest memory I struggled with my belief that I didn't belong in the world; that I wasn't deserving of unconditional love, that I would be abandoned by all who claimed to care. I don't recall the moment I realised that I was different or felt I did not belong in my family, I just always knew. My core belief was that I was not worthy of my biological father's love – that he did not love me enough to '*not die*.' Logically, I knew he did not choose his death, but the fact remains that his early departure from my life left a huge chasm in my soul – one that would detrimentally alter my self-worth.

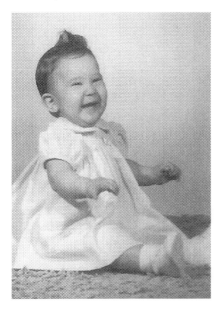

My story begins with the love of Jane and John, my biological parents. Young, in love and recently married, they started their family with my birth. As the result of their devotion, they doted on me and showered me with love and affection. My Father apprenticed as an accountant, working towards his CA designation and was required to travel often out of the country, leaving Mom with the sole responsibility of my care. Tragically, my Father was killed in a plane crash on one of his frequent trips to Montana when I was only four months old, leaving my Mom a widow at the age of twenty-one. The sudden loss of her husband undoubtedly affected Mom in many ways, including her perception of me. Years later, watching my descent into anorexia brought to the forefront her fear of my imminent death.

Somehow Mom found the strength to carry on, and went back to work teaching, leaving me in the care of my Baba. Life was difficult for her, but being twice fortunate she met a wonderful man and they married a couple years later. Not only did he commit his life and love to Mom, but he also accepted me with an open heart. It may have been difficult at times to step into a ready-made family, but their love for each other and their young daughter sealed their commitment. Over a span of nine years they added three more children to our family, providing me with all the joy siblings bring into one's life.

My desperate quest for unconditional love and acceptance began as a young girl. My earliest memory, at age 2 ½, is of their wedding, with me sneaking up to the Head Table in hopes of inclusion – as I had been assigned to a different table in my Aunt's care. From that moment on I felt like an alien, peering in from the outside.

My parents love me, I know they loved me to the best of their ability – and all their actions came from a place of love, never judgement - but they could only give me what they themselves were given. I am neither judge nor jury and my purpose is not to condemn. Perhaps the mistake my parents made was maintaining my separateness within the family unit, which I believe was done to honour my birth Father's memory. Whether held-up in the court system or perhaps delayed by my parents, my formal adoption by my (step) Father did not occur until three years after their marriage, and I began Kindergarten in the middle of the 'alphabetical line-up' (with a last name beginning with 'K') only to finish off the year at the beginning of this line (with a last name beginning with 'B'). For three of my formative years my surname was different than the rest of my family, and even after my formal adoption I still felt separated from my family because of the two last names on my birth certificate. I was questioned and ridiculed by my teammates every year at softball registration. I still hear their laughter which followed their comments of *"what kind of a stupid name is that?"*

Many memories of my early childhood remain strong. They were monumental in the discord of my spirit and set the stage for a life of depression, anxiety and eventually an eating disorder. I grew up not knowing half of my heritage – not knowing who the total sum of myself really was. My biological Father was an only child, his Mother died when he was fourteen, and his Father, my Grandpa, moved to another province after my Father died. My parents made great efforts to keep Grandpa K a close part of my life. We took many trips out to British Columbia to visit him, and he came to stay with us each summer, until his passing when I was twelve years old. I missed a casual and more consistent relationship with him though. I had no close relatives to share stories of my Father – who he was or what he was like – and I was consequently left paternally void. My feelings that I did not belong in my 'new family' was tragic; knowing only half of who I was became devastating. The despair I carried over the loss of my biological Father overpowered me at the mere mention of his name, the tight knot of grief overflowing with the tears running down my face – grief and despair that set me apart from everyone else. I was embarrassed and thought *"who am I to shed tears for this man? What right do I have to cry for someone I didn't even know?"* And yet that is exactly why I cried, because the birthright of a relationship with my Father was stolen from me.

For many years I had an imaginary family that I would 'live with.' Most nights after I went to bed I would lay awake for hours pretending to be in my 'perfect family'. This family consisted of my biological Mom and Dad, Jane and John, two older brothers – Cory (which would have been my name if I was born a boy) and Johnny, an older sister Brenda (who was *not* me – I feel it is noteworthy that I chose not to be the 'Brenda' in my pretend family), me – Kandi (think for a moment on the significance of the name I chose for myself...Kandi, something that is sweet and desirable and that everyone loves), and a younger sister and baby brother – Stacey and Paul. I placed myself in the middle of the family birth order, surrounding myself with love on both sides. In this pretend family we all got along and we all <u>belonged</u>. Love and respect guided all we did together. In my nightly imaginings I would play out typical events in family life – school, vacations, outings and meals to name a few. I anticipated my private time with my pretend family all day long, and this aided me in ignoring the reality of my true existence and got me through my tortured moments. I never shared my pretend family with anyone, I held them close to my heart, they were mine and mine alone. They were a strategic coping mechanism that guided me through my unhappy childhood.

Perfectionism was emphasized in my family and I attempted to win my parents' unconditional love and my rightful place in this new family by excelling in all I attempted. However, no matter how hard I tried or how well I performed, it was never adequate in my heart. My parents were proud of me and commended me on all my accomplishments, but they left no room for just 'good enough.' Ballet exams brought on anxiety attacks as early as age eight and caused me to lay awake most of the night sobbing for weeks prior. I drove myself to excel in piano, practicing for up to four hours a day prior to the Royal Conservatory exams. I was always the nerd in school, standing out from my friends with my academic achievements. I cried and I prayed nightly to be 'just an ordinary kid.' Hurtful incidents exacerbated over time resulting in an undiagnosed yet severe bout of depression by age thirteen. Years of being victimized by bullies took a huge toll on my self-esteem. I feared my daily walks to and from school as the only classmates who lived close to me and walked the same direction were a group of boys who tormented me verbally and physically.

Often I hid (in embarrassment) my muddy or grass-stained pants in the laundry as soon as I got home from school because 'the George boys' would knock me down and drag me across the school field. In the winter months I was pelted with icy snowballs and taunted by the chorus of *"teacher's pet, teacher's pet!"* I soon learnt to not bother telling my teachers about this torment as I was quickly dismissed and told to *"just ignore them, they are just jealous."* Being the so-called 'object of envy' was my daily curse.

I was truly miserable, whether I was at school or at home. My (step) Father took the stance of the bystander within the role of disciplinarian and at times I was grateful for this. They believed they were doing what was best for me, however I often overheard Dad say to Mom *"she's your daughter, you deal with her,"* which once again would cause me to feel that I was set apart from the other kids.

My 'bestest friend' and confidante, my cousin Michele, and I collected all types of frog/toad figurines in our childhood. They were our typification – we talked in voices replicating 'Kermit the Frog' from Sesame Street, we caught and raced toads every weekend we spent camping with our parents, we gave each other 'frog piggy banks' or T-shirts with stylized frog/toad designs for birthdays. I never questioned my affinity with these creatures…for some reason I related to them on a very basic level. I believe that they represented to me the ability to change into a form different than how they began life – transforming from an insignificant tadpole swimming aimlessly through the water to a revised life form, now able to live and breathe with developed mobility in a wholly different environment – not unlike my desire to change from the sad outcast I embodied to a new entity that was loved, and truly belonged.

I look back on junior high school as the most depressing years of my childhood. Dad was the Principal of one of the feeder schools to my junior high school, and I found myself in the same classes as some of his former students. I was derisively referred to as *"Mr. B's kid,"* and even though they respected him as their former principal, they did not feel it was 'cool' to admit it. It was much easier to bully his daughter. The teachers in my school all knew my Dad, and treated me differently than the other students. And the one thing that can ruin a child's school experience is being treated differently than others. I tried my hardest to fit in – I joined all the school teams and I did have a couple of close friends – yet I found myself drifting from one group of classmates to another, always searching for a place to belong.

The beginning of high school saw my transformation from 'ugly duckling to beautiful swan.' Contact lenses replaced glasses, and I found I no longer stood out academically, as there were many other 'smart kids' in my new school. I still felt the need to strive for perfect grades but this was tempered by my new-found social status as a popular girl. However, my fear of abandonment tainted all my relationships – I had vowed early in my life to never again place myself in a position where someone I cared about could leave me. At the first sign of romantic discord I quickly broke off the relationship claiming the role of 'abandon-er.' In addition to this, I valued myself in relation to my 'current boyfriend.' I aimed high and dated only the coolest, the cutest, the richest - but never the smartest - as that would have emphasized in me that which I aimed to ignore. My self-worth was directly proportionate to the perceived value of my boyfriend. I had to have plans for both nights of every weekend to prevent me from falling into a downhill spiral of self-condemnation and hatred.

My teenage years were rebellious…I figured that if I could not <u>fit in</u> then I would <u>stand out</u>. I wanted to be noticed, and negative attention was as effective as, if not better than, positive attention. I had to prove to (myself and) others that I was not that unloved, unwanted and unnecessary girl that I thought I was. Although I never got into serious trouble with the law, I broke many of the rules my parents enforced. I was fulfilling my self-prophecy of being the outsider and doing all I could to prove that I was cool and worthy of (peer-pressuring) friends.

With no knowledge (at the time) of why I was afflicted with an eating disorder, my parents searched for a concrete reason in an attempt to understand the craziness that had enveloped their lives. Both of them related it back to a situation from grade twelve when my school volleyball team participated in an out-of-town tournament. In my mind, this was simply an opportunity to act out against the authority of our coaches/chaperones, and had no bearing on the on-set of anorexia that began over a year later. However, for years both Mom and Dad blamed the decision the senior girls on the team made to bring along hash as the first step in my anorexic decline. This is an extreme example of how anorexia may be trivialized into one single event, without the knowledge of its deep-seated roots. There is never one reason nor incident that causes the on-set of this disease – but rather a culmination of hurts built up over time in conjunction with long-term negative feelings in the sufferer.

In retrospect – reviewing my life as an observer watching a movie screen – I can now distance myself from my earlier damaged psyche and attempt to analyze my descent into anorexic hell from an objective point of view. My recent journey of the self-discovery of my true essence has encouraged me to break a destructive cycle of depression and anxiety that may have affected generations of my family. I no longer view therapy as a sign of weakness but see it as one of the strongest and most loving decisions I can make. Surrendering (by seeking and accepting help) is <u>not</u> about giving up in defeat – it is being enlightened enough to realize that I cannot change the universe nor how others react to it. I am only responsible for my actions and reactions. I view surrender as giving up my control, which in turn, brings me inner peace and happiness.

"Faith is the daring of the soul to go farther than it can see."
William Newton Clarke

Once I left for university and was out of the constant watch of my parents, the toxic combination of my continuous quest for unconditional love and acceptance, along with my drive for perfection, created the perfect storm for the entrenchment of anorexia. I was the quintessential candidate to develop an eating disorder and once the foundation was laid, the storm quickly sent me on a disastrous journey....

This...is the beginning

My story took roots as a fourteen year old girl who portrayed everything positive on the outside but was plagued with the darkness of a lost soul filled with self-loathing. I always felt like a pariah, never fitting in with family nor friends, forever an outcast. I suffered from a dark depression for as long as I could remember. My public persona was perfect and I excelled at everything I undertook. An honour student, an above average pianist, the star of the fastball team, and the virtuoso of my strict ballet teacher. Perfectionism was my driver, and I refused to fail at anything.

As a young teenage girl, I was babysitting my younger cousins one Saturday night. Once all my chores were complete, and the kids asleep in their beds, I decided to pull out the new book I had just borrowed from the library and spend the rest of the evening indulging in my favourite past-time. I was intrigued by the title of the book and looked forward to cuddling up under the blankets on the sofa while I awaited my aunt and uncle's return. My book of choice that evening was a fictional story of a young girl suffering from anorexia nervosa – an illness little acknowledged and even less understood at the time. The title of the book was "The Best Little Girl in the World," and as I sat all alone in the dimly lit living room, I was grazed by the chilling talons of the disease. An ominous voice whispered a message to me which would take years to manifest > **WOW, IT WOULD BE GREAT TO HAVE THIS DISEASE...TO HAVE CONTROL OVER EVERYTHING...AND EVERYONE WOULD WORRY FOR ME, AND LOVE ME <**

Fast forward four years and I was a successful eighteen year old in my first year of university, living in residence with lots of friends, studying my passion and dating the BMOC – Big Man On Campus. I was the envy of many. But an off-hand, and seemingly innocent, remark from the love of my life would rekindle the flames of despair within my soul and careen me down a dark and tragic path.

I had unfortunately gained the typical ten pounds in my first year living in university residence. Eating the starchy food and not maintaining the active lifestyle that I had in high school had resulted in what my boyfriend casually dubbed my *"Dairy Queen legs,"* which I perceived as his disgust with my fat thighs; yet looking back now, I realise was meant as a term of endearment. I made the vow to myself to return to the tall, slim and desirable young woman I started university as – the one who caught JT's eye. I cut out all dairy products,  carbohydrates/starches and meat from my diet, and started a rigorous exercise regime. I was not alone in my quest to lose weight. Residence was full of (mostly) girls who felt they were not their ideal weight. There was an undercurrent of competition to be the prettiest and the thinnest. As now, the media at that time glorified slim physiques, and the exercise craze of the 'eighties' was exemplified in movies and magazines. However, being the perfectionist that I was, I was determined to lose the weight quicker and more successfully than any of my fellow co-eds.

I pursued my quest easily throughout my summer back home with my family, typically staying under the radar of their concern. I would claim I worked one hour later than I actually did and snuck a five mile run in before going home. It was easy to say that I was meeting friends for dinner to get out of having to join my family for the evening meal, thereby allowing myself time to also fit in an aerobics dance class along with my daily run. The extra pounds were easily dropped, and this so encouraged me that I decided I should lose extra weight to combat any I may gain back upon my return to residence for my second year.. **> SO YOU LOST A COUPLE POUNDS...BIG DEAL...YOU'RE STILL SUCH A FAT PIG AND WILL GAIN THEM ALL BACK...THEN WHO WILL LOVE YOU...NOBODY... NOBODY LOVES YOU <**

I had the perfect summer job working in an office with many (male) engineering students. My summer goal of physical perfection was driven by my need to be invited into this group of desirable young men! I was faithful to my boyfriend JT – at the time I thought that he was my true love - but I needed the constant affirmation of my attractiveness and enjoyed the attention these guys showed me. Every weekend was spent partying with my new friends, or going out dancing at the clubs and having all my drinks paid for.

DEMON thought he was cunning enough to have duped my parents and I thought I was sailing through my summer back home, keeping my dark secret hidden. Mom is a very perceptive person – like most mothers are – and she realised something was not quite right. Thinking my weight-loss and exacerbated isolation from my family was depression-driven (which I suppose it partially was), she tearfully requested that I meet with a psychiatrist. After only a couple of sessions, Dr. L. convinced her that I needed to be hospitalized. I agreed, DEMON laughing inside me, proud of the fact that my eating disorder was concealed and the emphasis was placed on depression. **> WOW ARE THESE PEOPLE EVER STUPID...THEY CAN'T SEE WHAT'S RIGHT IN FRONT OF THEM <** I viewed my impending week in the hospital as a holiday from work and pranced onto the psych ward with a gleam in my eye and strategy in my heart. Once admitted, I was easily lost in the shuffle of the more serious cases and could pretty much do as I wanted. I was not placed under the same restrictions as the other psych patients, as I was not considered a threat to myself or others. I had to put up with a couple of consultations with Dr. L., but he was not as tuned in to me as he was with his other responsibilities, and DEMON humoured his weak requirements of me. The anti-depressant medication I was given was hidden under my tongue and quickly spit in the toilet once the nurse left my room. **> YOU DON'T NEED THIS SHIT...IT WILL TAKE AWAY YOUR CONTROL...BE STRONG...SPIT IT OUT <**

This was also the time that I decided to take up smoking. Everyone on the psych ward smoked and I quickly realised that cigarettes would temporarily stave off any feelings of hunger. I was sitting in the lounge up on the ward visiting with the other patients watching TV and having a cigarette one afternoon when my Mom popped in for an unexpected visit. As soon as I saw her round the corner I threw my cigarette into the ashtray, hoping I had managed to conceal it from her. I am unsure if I was successful, but she did not say anything about it to me. Mom was quite efficient by that point at ignoring things she did not want to know about. DEMON picked up on this and was encouraged in his efforts to mislead her in the future. **>HA...YOU GOT AWAY WITH THIS...SHE'LL NEVER FIGURE THINGS OUT <**

I was very friendly and jovial during my time in the hospital, as I had to prove that I was not suffering from depression, and made friends with a number of the patients. One girl, Barb, was close to my age and was in the hospital because of a suicide attempt. We became close and were the two radicals on the ward, quietly breaking any rule that we could. **> YOU DON'T HAVE TO LISTEN TO THEM... THEY DON'T CONTROL YOU...YOU CONTROL THEM...GO <** We even managed to escape the confines of the hospital a couple of times and spend a few hours roaming free at the mall across the street from the hospital. Patients on the psych ward were allowed to wear regular clothes if they wished - there were no requirements for the hospital gowns as on other wards - and Barb and I would disappear stealthily down the stairwell and out the front entrance of the hospital. Obviously this hospital stay was not effective at all for my recovery, and Dr. L. discharged me a week later with *"no sign of my previous depression apparent."* I went back to work, no-one the wiser as to where I spent my 'vacation,' and I resumed life as I knew it.

Upon my return to university for year two, my determination and efforts to lose weight were rewarded by JT's renewed commitment to our relationship, as well as compliments cast my way by other guys; **> TOLD YOU HE WOULD ONLY LOVE YOU IF YOU ARE SKINNY <** but even more so by the (mostly) covert glares of jealousy from the other girls. I was winning the (furtive) competition; I was the slimmest, the most successful dieter, the most desirable!

However, with every mile run – I was now up to ten miles a day, run mostly during the late night hours around the dark university campus – and with every pound dropped, the more entrenched in this disease I became. It was getting so difficult to concentrate on my studies with my mind being consumed with thoughts of food and DEMON'S negative comments. The voices in my head were relentless, and I never had a chance to think thoughts of my own choice. Both body and mind had been taken over by this disease, and my spirit was crushed. I was constantly planning what was 'safe' to eat, how many calories I would be forced to ingest, and how many extra miles I would have to run to work them off. I knew the caloric count of everything, from a baked potato to a glass of milk to a piece of licorice. I relied on cigarettes and Diet Coke to carry me through the hunger pains. JT and some close friends noticed not only my continued weight loss but also a change in my personality. I was very moody and quick to anger or tears. I was always cold, dressed in layers of baggy clothing to hide my physique, which I justified by the cold winter weather. My 'manageable' decline in weight and descent into my personal hell was still mostly hidden though, or so I thought…

My first intervention happened when my RA (Residents' Assistant) Shelley invited me into her room for a 'chat.' Waiting for me were three of my closest friends who quickly bombarded me with questions and concern. They were worried about how little I was eating, about my solo, late-night runs around the university campus and my growing seclusion from 'the group.' I almost, *almost*, gave in and admitted my fear of what was happening to me, but DEMON quickly took control of the situation **> THEY DON'T UNDERSTAND...THEY WILL MAKE YOU EAT...THEY WANT YOU TO BE FAT...DON'T LISTEN TO THEM <** and I turned on the tears and explained it all away as the stress of university life.

A couple of my close friends from high school, Val and Joanne, came for a visit during their Reading Week at University of Alberta. I had a wonderful time introducing them to my friends, and they got a great taste of residence life. What mostly stands out for me though was Joanne bringing me a pair of jeans from back home that I hadn't fit in since I last wore them in high school. They were one of my favourite jeans and I was anxious to have them with me at university, and was excited to see if I had lost enough weight to fit in to them again. I remember trying them on and they literally fell off me...they were way too big! DEMON was so proud of me and I basked in the glow of my (over) accomplishment. It was with great pride that I handed the jeans back to Joanne to return to my home, and I decided that the three of us needed to go on a shopping spree before they left. After all, I had worked very hard and was so committed to losing weight that I needed to show off my new figure in skin-tight jeans. **> SIZE 3?? YOU FAT PIG...WHO WILL LOVE YOU NOW? <**

My quest for popularity culminated near the end of second year with my decision to run for President of the Residence Students' Union. I campaigned diligently and was rewarded with a landslide victory over my opponents. This was another affirmation by DEMON that I was doing the right thing... skinniest = most popular = President! This was a coveted position as all the students knew the President and looked upon her as the 'Queen of Rez.' I was walking on clouds and had an amazing third year to look forward to. This win caused me to change my earlier plans of moving out of residence and into an apartment with JT and his sister, whom I was close friends with. **> THEY WILL TAKE AWAY YOUR CONTROL... THEY DON'T LOVE YOU...THEY JUST WANT YOU FAT SO THEY CAN LEAVE YOU <** This became a significant turning point in my decline. I believe that staying in residence for a third year exacerbated my decline and if I would have stayed with my initial plan of moving out, the anorexia may not have kept such a strong hold on me nor progressed as far as it did.

'Color Night' was the big formal event in residence, honouring the out-going Student Executive Committee and welcoming the incoming. This was to be my big event and I was very much looking forward to it as this was my moment to shine! However, I would soon see that my 'gravy train' could derail...and disastrously!

Thinking back on this night, I have to remind myself that my brain was so pre-occupied with thoughts of food that I wasn't thinking rationally. Of course, being a university event, the beer was flowing steadily and I had 'pre-partied' extensively before the formal evening began. And being a light-weight (literally), it didn't take much to become inebriated. At one point during the festivities, I saw *my* JT dancing with another girl. **> TOLD YOU THAT YOU ARE TOO FAT AND UGLY...HE DOESN'T LOVE YOU...HE WOULD NEVER LOVE A PIG <** Now this was not tragic in itself, as it was quite common for guys and girls to dance together even if they weren't boyfriend/girlfriend, but I was furious and lost any rational part of my brain that was still functioning. I ran up to him, slapped him across the face, flung the diamond promise ring he had given me the previous Christmas, and ran off the dance floor in tears, making an absolute spectacle of us both. But I didn't stop there. I ran back to my room, grabbed JT's sweatshirt and a glass of water, and went into the stairwell to light his shirt on fire. **> SHOW HIM WHO CONTROLS WHO <** Imagine the look of horror on the face of the shy Asian student as she ascended the stairs and came across the maniacal new president, standing over a piece of burning clothing holding a glass of water in case the fire got out of control!

Once the sweatshirt was nothing but a pile of charred remains I calmly walked away, almost as if in a trance, and went back to my room and passed out. I obviously wasn't thinking clearly, or thinking at all, because I left the evidence of my insanity in the stairwell. Upon awakening late the next morning I sat up with fear and dread in my heart that not only would I be relieved of my position as President and kicked out of residence, but perhaps even dismissed from the university. Running out to the stairwell however, I saw no remnants of the fire and over the next few days, nothing was ever said to me. I never found out who cleaned it up – either my Angels were looking out for me, or DEMON was protecting itself.

I returned back home to my family that April (at the end of my second year of university) as a skeleton of the person I left as eight months earlier. Totally entrenched now in the disease, I no longer cared to hide it from anyone…in fact, I was proud! I had managed to get down from my original 142 pounds on my 5'7" frame to about 110 pounds – a loss of 25 percent of my body weight. Still though, that was not good enough for DEMON. That 99 pound mark was so close and I felt like a failure until I could reach double digits. I ignored all the signs of my destruction – the demise of a couple of close friendships, **> SO WHAT…THEY DON'T LOVE YOU…YOU ARE**

DISGUSTING...NOBODY COULD LOVE A COW < the screaming tantrums targeted at my parents, the tears shed at any given moment, the decreasing ability to concentrate, and the cold...I was always so cold. The heat of the summer months no longer afforded me the excuse for bulky layers.

I managed to hold down a full-time summer job at the same office as the previous summer and continued my rigorous exercise regime on less and less food. I surpassed the point of being in control though. Somehow the reigns had been stolen from me and the dark DEMON took complete control of my mind and body. There were the odd lucid moments when I was able to view myself from the outside, but these moments brought such disgust and fear that I quickly turned back inside myself. This summer I was no longer the confident and popular girl in the office and the guys tended to stay away from me. No-one knew how to deal with this 'too thin' girl, who spent her lunch hour running off the calories of the sugar she put in her coffee. I was existing in a cocoon, ignoring the stares and comments of my co-workers. **> THEY DON'T UNDERSTAND...YOU CONTROL THEM...THEY DON'T EVEN WANT TO KNOW YOU <**

A moment of truth hit me about halfway through the summer. I remember having an okay day at work, keeping DEMON away for the most part. I even chose to abandon my daily run and aerobics class to join my family for dinner. But as soon as I sat down at the table the attention everyone put on me and the expectations of eating a full meal with them sent me in a tailspin. **> SHOW THEM...YOU CONTROL...THEY DON'T... THEY CAN'T LOVE A FAT STUPID PIG...WHY SHOULD YOU EVEN LIVE...YOU'RE DISGUSTING... YOU NEVER SHOULD HAVE BEEN BORN <** The unseen tension cracked, the accusations flew and tears were spilt.

Many horrible words were shouted that caused great hurt to all. I ran up to my room, blasted Billy Joel's "My Life" and overdosed on Extra Strength Tylenol. My Mom came up to talk to me after a couple of hours and found me unconscious. It seemed that her premonition of losing me may come true.

I was rushed to the hospital and awoke to my stomach being pumped and surrounded by the harsh faces of the hospital staff – there was no compassion for suicide attempts. My eating disorder was discussed – *"who me? An eating disorder? No way! I was just so pissed at my parents!"* and I was admitted into the Psych Ward (of a different hospital than the previous summer). This was definitely not the place I planned to spend much time. I was still quite good at manipulating my Mom and I convinced her into having me discharged after only a couple of days. DEMON turned on the tears and the guilt trip and I promised to stop exercising and start eating. I was even able to choke down a banana as proof of the new me. That 'new me' didn't last long though, only until I woke up in my own bed the following morning with DEMON even stronger inside me.

Looking back years later, I was so ashamed of how I manipulated my Mom, allowing her false hope that was short-lived. Now that I am a mother myself, I can only imagine her pain from the white-hot knife I kept twisting in her heart. She had lost her first husband, my biological Father, four months after my birth and now she was watching, with no control, her first born starving herself to death. And I had no thoughts on how this episode would burn itself indelibly into the memory of my younger siblings. To this day my precious 'baby brother,' now forty years old, vividly remembers the tragic confusion of that evening. Hiding with my sister, out of the way of the paramedics, the revolving light of the ambulance illuminating our cul-de-sac like a beacon, being left alone with his older siblings as my parents accompanied me to the hospital…the fear and uncertainty of what would happen to Brenda…*"would she ever come back home?"*

Another disconcerting result of my suicide attempt was the loss of one of my best friends. Joanne was at a loss as to how to deal with my altered personality and decided that it was in the best interest of her own emotional health to cut ties with me. **> SEE…NO-ONE LOVES YOU…NOT EVEN YOUR BEST FRIEND <** I was very hurt and angry at her dismissal of a five-year friendship, and what I viewed as her desertion of me. As with other important people in my life, I did not focus on how DEMON was affecting them; I was solely centered on myself and my quest to control. When others made decisions that I did not agree with and that hurt me, I dismissed them, ignoring their importance in my life.

My eating disorder was pretty much out in the open now and extended family and friends were aware of what was happening to me and how it was affecting my family. Many of my relatives attempted to lovingly intervene…my Baba promised to take me shopping if I would only start eating; my Aunty Kathy took me out and attempted to talk some sense into me while convincing me to share drinks and chicken fingers with her; my Aunty Marcia asked me why I would throw away my promising life – *"how can such a smart and beautiful girl do this to herself?"* And of course there was always the negative 'guilt trip,' desperately attempted by anyone and everyone – *"why are you hurting your Mom like this?"* **> I DON'T CARE, SHE HURTS ME <** *"Can't you see how worried she is?"* **> NO SHE ISN'T…SHE'S JUST PRETENDING…SHE NEVER LOVED ME <** *"Why are you being so selfish?"* **> BECAUSE I AM A BITCH <** *"Just eat!"* **> I CAN'T!!!! <**

It was at this time that it really hit JT how serious the situation had become. He sent me flowers when I got out of the hospital and I mailed him a picture of me with the flowers. When he received my card and picture in the mail, he was shocked at the skeletal figure his girlfriend had become. This was the point he realised that anorexia had truly taken hold of me, and it was beyond his power to stop it. He felt very much in the dark and that there was not much information readily available – there was no internet back then. And this was a time that mental illnesses were not discussed, they were very much taboo. He realised there was no easy fix, no medicine available to make it go away. There was much uncertainty in his mind, and he was not confident enough with his knowledge of the disease to confront me. He did not feel that he was mature enough to handle the effects of my illness, and wished that he would have asked more questions of me and had more communication with my family, instead of feeling solely responsible for health and recovery during the university year.

My younger sister Sanny had idolized me her whole life and in her eyes I could do no wrong, or so she thought. She is nine years younger than I am and was at a very influential age when I started my downhill spiral. She unfailingly supported me when my parents lost patience with my ludicrous behaviour. She defended all I did and was always available with hugs and support when I opened up to her. I selfishly never worried about my negative influence on her, because I needed her positive support. She would ride her bike alongside me when I went for my runs, and she was my shopping companion, never uttering a negative word, even when I was fitting into girl-sized clothes. **> FAT COW <** Although many times I would question and fear my negative influence on her, I was so focused on myself and my determination to dwell in my DEMON'S cave that I could not summon the strength to change things. **> SHE DOESN'T LOVE YOU...SHE WANTS YOU TO**

DIE...SHE'S THE SPECIAL ONE...YOU'LL NEVER BE SPECIAL TO ANYONE < My parents did their best to shelter her from my experience, but the closeness Sanny and I shared often circumvented their efforts. I am so grateful that DEMON never set his sights on her, but kept his debilitating focus on me. However, Sanny truly filled the role of the 'silent sufferer' in all this.

Although Dr. B. recommended – and we attempted – family counselling sessions, they did not always have the desired outcome for my family. Many fresh hurts and long-standing grievances were shared but it was difficult for all of us to face the anger and hurt evident in our family. Because of this, we didn't complete enough sessions to gain any benefit from this form of counselling. Our final session had the most negative impact, leaving a tragic and lasting memory. I didn't recall the details of this meeting until discussing it years later – my mind blocked this memory in an attempt to heal – but not so for the others. Sanny recalls a very upsetting session with everyone yelling and blaming my eating disorder and my consequent actions for all our issues. At one point I had had enough and stormed out of the room screaming that I was never coming back (to family counselling). Ever my defender and supporter, Sanny ran after me to hug and comfort me as I sobbed and raged against Dr. B. and our parents. I am unaware of how the meeting ended, but Dad recently shared with me that he felt a great amount of guilt for what I was going through and thought it best for the family well-being if he and Mom split up. Luckily, they resolved their negative feelings and our family remained intact. Unfortunately, it is not uncommon for the parents of an eating disorder sufferer to blame each other, or blame themselves, causing the tragic break-up of the family.

My brother Greg recalls a different episode that remains vivid for him. Unbeknownst by others, he partially overheard an emotional exchange between Dad and myself, which he has wondered about for years but never had the courage to question. Dad and I were arguing, and at one point he broke down in tears. Dad was not one to show his vulnerability and throughout our childhood we rarely, if ever, saw him cry. This time though, he could not contain his grief and the tears flowed freely.

It amazes me, after speaking with each of the people closest to me at the time, how everyone's perspective of my decline is so different; we all remember certain events quite clearly while others were forgotten – graciously blocked from our memories.

The highlight of that summer was JT visiting me from his hometown in Ontario. We had a blissful week together thanks to his ability to ignore the fact I was not eating, that I was thinner than when he last saw me a couple months back, and that at any given moment I could either break down in tears or erupt in anger, with no warning nor justification. But his strong arms were there to hold me, and his soft lips were there to kiss away my tears, until DEMON inevitably pushed him away. JT played the role of my knight in shining armour, my rescuer, and my protector. But not even he could outwit nor out maneuver DEMON. JT proposed to me that week amidst the majesty of the Rocky Mountains. DEMON teased me with a few moments of basking in JT's love and planning a promising future together. But when JT left to return to his home for the remainder of the summer, DEMON was back...in full force **> YOU ARE FREE...HE'LL NEVER KNOW... HE DOESN'T WANT YOU ANYWAY...HE DOESN'T LOVE YOU <**

I started off third year of university on top of my world. I had cracked the 100 pound mark and proudly showed off my 98 pound physique in some new form-fitting fashions that I had splurged on that summer. I was the most popular girl – being President of the Residence Student Association, everyone knew my name and face, and shared smiles and 'hellos' passing in the hallway. My studies were suffering however, due to my lack of brain concentration as well as the required social activities my position required. DEMON justified my dropping a few courses

which would require an extra year at university by allowing me to bask in the glory of my weight-control success. JT was very concerned however, and shared his fears with my Mom. To alleviate their concerns – and basically get them off my case – I agreed to an out-patient program at the University of Winnipeg hospital. **> JUST PLAY ALONG...SOON THEY WILL FORGET YOU...YOU CONTROL <** JT accompanied me to my weekly weigh-ins and psychologist appointments. I was still losing pounds very quickly but figured out that I could disguise this by wearing ankle weights, hidden by my pant legs, to my weigh-ins. My brain may not have been working well in classes but it certainly rose to the occasion when I had to dupe those whose love and concern would have attempted to 'control my control'.

My exercise regime, consisting of my nightly run, was enhanced by an hour swim before classes each morning. My diet consisted of diet Coke, coffee, cigarettes and the odd salad. Very rarely I would indulge in a couple handfuls of popcorn – no butter – during an evening study session. I would feel so guilty, so <u>fat</u>, afterward that I would increase my run on those particular nights to twice my typical circuit. **>LOSER... SWINE...YOU CAN'T DO ANYTHING RIGHT <**

The Friday before Thanksgiving weekend started off as most other Friday nights in residence – pre-partying before the scheduled residence event and then attending the organised dance social. This night would end up being one of the turning points in my life; the moment that changed the course of my illness, my future with JT, and my university experience. I was partying with my friends and having a great time dancing to the music when my body suddenly gave out. I collapsed, momentarily unconscious, and had to be brought back to my room. A very worried JT called my Mom and expressed his grave concern over my declining health. I thought I had convinced him that I was okay and life would continue as it had. However, my Mom called me the next day and told me that she was flying out the next weekend to bring me home for treatment. The determined tone in her voice broke through my fog, and I knew that if I didn't go home and accept help I would not live long. The next week was so emotionally challenging for me, not only did I have to withdraw from university and resign from my highly acclaimed position as President, **> NOBODY WANTS YOU HERE ANYWAY...THEY HATE YOU...PIGGY <** but even harder was saying good-bye to all my friends in what I viewed as a state of disgrace. I didn't realize at the time that the good-byes I was wished were not motivated by disgust, but by love and concern. The vision of over fifty of my friends all standing outside the doors of the residence waving good-bye and blowing kisses as Mom and I drove away broke me, and sobs of sorrow racked my body. My Mom had to take over driving as I was overcome with shame and failure. The sixteen hours spent driving across the barren prairies were spent mostly in silence. Both of our brains were busy chirping their own stories, **> THEY HATE YOU... NOBODY CARES...JUST DIE ALREADY <** but the words were frozen in our hearts without hope of release.

Back home, and back in my game, sort of…

This...*is my darkest hour*

Being forced back home from university was a telling moment for my family as well as for me. This was the memorable event that exemplified the seriousness of my situation to all, regardless of their age. My parents offered an explanation to my siblings that was age-appropriate for each of them, offering only the information that was required to explain why I was back from university on more permanent terms. My physical and emotional state emphasized that I needed more assistance than I had been receiving. Although I may not have seemed receptive, my siblings' attempts at support and understanding meant the world to me.

I had conceded to twice weekly sessions with a new psychiatrist who specialized in eating disorders and the scrutinizing care of a medical doctor. However, my terms were that I got to work full-time at (believe it or not) an eating establishment. I also insisted that I was in control of what and how much I ate and that I could maintain my exercise regime. I viewed my psychiatrist, Dr. B., as a pompous jerk with the requisite book smarts but no idea of what living with anorexia was all about. He would sit back in his big black chair, behind his big black desk, with his big stomach spilling into his lap, and insist I was depressed, and he would try to convince me that I needed depression meds. There was no way I would agree to this, I saw firsthand what those meds did to people during my brief stays on the psych ward **> THOSE DRUGGED UP ZOMBIES DO NOTHING BUT LAY AROUND ALL DAY AND GET FAT! <** My medical doctor wasn't falling for my tricks though; he insisted that I strip down to my underwear for my weekly weigh-ins. It was impossible for me to wear ankle weights or hide my rock-filled pockets under bulky sweatshirts. I was physically failing very quickly at this point, and I don't know where the pounds I continually lost came from. I weighed in at about 72 pounds by November, half of my body weight from 1 ½ years prior.

My typical day consisted of working an eight-hour shift at the restaurant carrying trays laden with platters of food and jugs of beer, going for a run before heading home (I could only manage two miles at that point) and collapsing into bed. **> GET UP YOU FAT COW...YOU ARE SO USELESS <** I was nourishing my body with one can of Ensure (250 calories) a day and ever since have credited this nutrient-packed supplement for keeping me alive. It was one of the coldest winters in Edmonton that year and I was always so cold, dressed in layers of bulky sweaters and blasting the heat in my car and my bedroom.

My social life was basically non-existent. I had no energy to put into making new friends at the restaurant and none of my high school friends wanted to spend time with me - I believed at the time that they just did not care about me anymore (flashback to my consistent thoughts of *'not good enough for love'*). But now I realise that I must have frightened them - they did not know how to deal with my ever-changing and volatile moods. A couple of times I went out with my co-workers, but never felt truly welcomed. I was one of those 'have to invites,' because everyone else was going. The evening would begin at a local pizza parlour; everyone would be enjoying the greasy, calorie-laden pizza **> HOW COULD THEY DO THIS... DON'T THEY KNOW HOW FATTENING PIZZA IS...DON'T THEY CARE HOW HUGE THEY'LL GET <** and I would be picking the celery, cucumber and tomatoes out of my 'side garden salad,' and eating a few lettuce leaves.

JT tried to maintain our relationship long distance and gave me positive encouragement to recover but DEMON held a grudge toward him and set his sharp talons upon my heart, squeezing the life out of my love for JT. I could not forgive him for making that fateful call to my Mom and precipitating my shameful departure from university. When he sent me a beautiful bouquet of two dozen roses to honour our two year anniversary, I stubbornly refused to accept them and threw them out in the cold to quickly freeze up and die, **> HE DOESN'T LOVE YOU...NO-ONE WILL EVER LOVE YOU <** not unlike my spirit that was dying inside of me. I wouldn't accept his phone call, wouldn't wish him a Happy Anniversary, wouldn't share any declarations of love. I wouldn't find out until years later how my actions that day completely shattered JT's heart. It forever changed our destiny, and my previous desire to spend the rest of my life as his wife would never come to be.

That November my friend Val got married. Although I was excited to be included in the celebration, I was reluctant to go by myself. There was no boyfriend in my life to escort me, so Val arranged for a guy we often hung out with in high school to take me, as he was also invited and without a date. Lawrence ignored me for the most part, embarrassed by my physical appearance and disappointed that I was not the vibrant, attractive 'party-girl' that he remembered from high school. > **YOU WERE NEVER PRETTY...AND NEVER POPULAR...THEY ALL LAUGHED AT YOU BEHIND YOUR BACK...YOU ARE A LOSER WITH NO FRIENDS...EVERYONE HATES YOU** < He hadn't seen me since graduation, and Val failed to apprise him of my declining situation. In the face of my dear friend's marital bliss and the recent demise of my relationship with JT, I sank even lower.

By the beginning of December I was down to 69 pounds and my energy almost completely depleted. I had lost all ability to do anything but lay in bed, covered in masses of blankets. But even that was difficult because it had become painful for my hips and shoulders due to the lack of cushioning on my bones. I was literally skin and bones. Not only was my body wasted away but my spirit was empty of any desire to go on. **>DIE...JUST DIE...END THE PAIN...YOU CAN'T DO ANYTHING RIGHT** < I had a disturbing nightmare one night, starring me at my funeral, with my devastated Mom throwing clumps of frozen dirt on my grave, and the disappointed spirit of my long-dead Father hovering over. The next day at my appointment with Dr. B. I finally agreed to let go of my control, put my trust in him, and be admitted into a lengthy in-patient treatment program at the hospital. But not until after the new year, as I wanted to spend the Christmas season at home. My parents and Dr. B. were so taken aback by my concession that they agreed to my timeline. *This was the momentous turning point in my recovery and the dream-state message from my Spirit Guide (my biological Father who had physically abandoned me twenty-one years earlier), and my Mom, was the instrumental reason for my survival.*

DEMON was ultimately in control however. I still had one month to see how absolutely low I could get my weight.

**> DON'T GIVE UP...YOU ARE ALMOST THERE...
WHO CARES IF YOU DIE...YOU HAVE TO BE
THE SKINNIEST...OTHERWISE YOU ARE THE
UGLIEST <** I still needed to prove I was the best, the most
successful dieter, the winner! Although I was an emaciated shell
of a person, that Christmas was one of the best. My family and
I had much to celebrate and anticipate; we were all living for
the upcoming day I would be admitted into the hospital and
take my first honest step toward recovery.

I had a moment of foresight that first evening in my 'self-
imposed hospital jail cell', and I asked my Mom to take a
picture of me in a bathing suit, showing my emaciated body
and soul-less eyes. This photo caught all my desolation and
despair, **> YOU WILL NEVER OUT POWER ME...I
WILL CONTROL YOU FOREVER...THERE IS NO
END TO YOUR PAIN <** forever immortalized. I do
not know what prompted me
to want this photo to be
taken - was it a 'trophy-shot'
to show how successful I was
at controlling, or would it
become my future 'scare-
tactic', portraying where I
never again wanted to be?

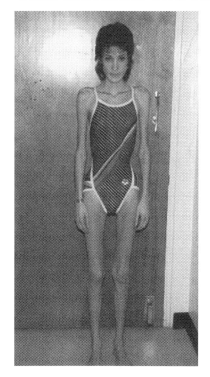

The evening I gave up
all control and was admitted
into the hospital was both
terrifying for me and
triumphant for my loving
parents. The next morning I
would begin my program and

relinquish all my strong convictions and demon-driven beliefs. I was a frantic soul, coerced into the unrelenting trap I felt others had placed upon me. All I had left was my faith, and I knelt down on my skin and bone knees on the cold hospital floor beside my institutional bed and prayed to God, Mary and my Guardian Angel for strength. Sobs of anguish shook my body and my soul. My loving Dad, who I mistakenly viewed throughout my illness as an unrelenting, yet mostly silent and disapproving judge, showed his immense love and support for me by coming alone to the hospital that night to visit. Unfortunately for him, he walked in right in the middle of my sob-fest, and I was so embarrassed by his discovery of my moment of weakness that I jumped– actually more like dragged myself – up off my knees and screamed at him to get out of my room and out of my life! I suppose that maniacal outburst wasn't what he was expecting, but he handled himself with grace, declared his love for me, and quietly left. And I attempted to pound DEMON out of me, punching and kicking my bed with what little strength I had. I collapsed on the cold floor, spending the night curled up in a fetal position, spiritually and emotionally broken**. > LOSER...WHAT WILL HAPPEN NOW...THEY JUST WANT YOU FAT...FAT...FAT... AND THEN THEY'LL LEAVE YOU <**

7:00 am came much too quickly the next morning and the battery of blood tests, weigh-ins and consultations began in earnest. My weight that morning was my lowest – 63 pounds - and DEMON raised its taloned hand and 'high-fived' me in congratulations...I was down to forty-four percent of my original body weight, a loss of 79 pounds in twenty-one months.

This ...is my climb

My spirit was starting to break through the destructive influence of DEMON. A faint voice was whispering that this was my defining moment – I would turn my life around and bury this demon instead of my family burying my lifeless bones. Over the next few years I would look at my photo whenever DEMON attempted to once again control me, and my determination to beat this tragic disease would gain strength.

The dichotomy of those first days of my journey were confusing for me as well as for the medical team working with me. On any given day my inner determination may weaken but my body would step up to carry the flame of my struggles. On other days, my body would resist the nourishment, yet my spirit would rekindle my resolve. This was a time of great fear for me and great hope for my family. Mom never faltered in her belief that where there is will, there is a way; and through her strong faith and heartfelt prayers she consistently attempted to strengthen my will and help me to find my way. My family did their best to understand my reluctance to let go, and the struggles I was constantly dealing with, but they couldn't comprehend the height of the mountain I had committed to climb. But in turn, I could not understand the height of the mountain they had been <u>forced</u> to climb. I would jokingly pat my swollen belly and refer to it as my 'food baby,' but when alone I would punch it in frustration and rage against those supporting me. **> I HATE THIS...I HATE YOU...I HATE ME...I JUST WANT TO DIE <**

My recovery program was physically restricting; I was not allowed off the ward without a wheelchair, and my dedicated nurse was my constant meal companion, sitting with me for as long as I took eating my meals. This became a game for me, and I would cut my food into the tiniest pieces possible, taking longer and longer to eat, seeing how far I could stretch this time with her. I was reaching out for love and attention from whomever would offer it. Oftentimes I was met with resistance – a cold shoulder turned my way or an unwelcoming look shunning me from what I so desperately sought. **> SEE WHAT HAPPENS WHEN YOU ARE FAT... NOBODY EVEN LIKES YOU...NOBODY WANTS YOU AROUND <** The nurses on the psych ward did not have much experience dealing with a patient with anorexia, for the symptoms fell between that of medical and mental. It was imperative that my medical needs were addressed immediately, as my physical body was near death, however the mental blocks DEMON had in place added a whole new dimension to the mix. For some reason I am unaware of, I was never placed on intravenous nutrition nor a feeding tube, which was both a blessing and a curse. I am not sure if my mental state would have been able to cope with force-feeding through medical intervention. Losing that last bit of control would likely have been my final break mentally. However, the daily task of sitting in front of a plate of food and physically lifting the fork to my mouth, chewing, and forcing myself to swallow was not much easier.

My daily weigh-ins were very difficult; **> SWINE...FAT COW...DISGUSTING LOSER...YOU ARE PATHETIC**

< I dreaded that part of my morning routine the most. I found it hard to reverse my thinking of condemning the pounds gained to the new requirement of blessing them. It was much easier not knowing; I would turn my back before getting on the scale so I wouldn't see the number.

I came up with routines and favourite habits that helped me through the hard moments. Before all my meals I would disappear into my bathroom and smoke a cigarette – smoking was still permitted in hospitals at that time, at least on the psych ward – then gargle with spearmint-flavoured mouthwash, and say a quick prayer for strength and courage. As mentioned earlier, I would cut my food into tiny pieces and stretch the mealtime as long as possible. I would pace the halls trying to walk off my pent-up frustration of not being allowed unnecessary physical activity. I would lock myself in the bathroom and march or jog in place, my arms pumping, my knees lifting high and my head held proud of my cunning ability to dupe the nurses. >**THEY ARE SO STUPID...YOU CAN DO WHATEVER YOU WANT BECAUSE NOBODY REALLY CARES** < I was even able to hide behind the curtains surrounding my hospital bed and do leg lifts and sit ups. All this in a controlling protest by DEMON.

I was a pariah on the ward and referred to as the 'little anorexic' with derision. I had nothing in common with the other patients – they feared me and I feared them. My family was very supportive though, and I anticipated their visits with joy. Most of my extended family visited a few times throughout my hospital stay; my parents at least a couple of times each week. My dear Mom was so dedicated that she would quickly go home to make the family dinner after working all day and then rush over to the hospital to spend the evening with me. I don't believe there were many days that she missed. I was so grateful for her love and support and her undying faith in me and my recovery. She saw me at my best and she saw me at my worst. She celebrated my milestone achievements, held me when I sobbed in frustration, and bore the full onslaught of my maniacal rants. **> I HATE YOU...WHY ARE YOU DOING THIS...I WANT TO DIE...LEAVE ME ALONE <** She was truly my rock, and I love her with my entire being.

My recovery was slow but steady. The main focus was to get me back up to an 'acceptable unhealthy weight.' In other words, provide enough nourishment for my depleted body in order that my organs would not fail. This was an emotional climb for me, and I often felt that I looked six months pregnant with my swollen belly full of food in quantities it was not used to. The first couple weeks I had to carry a pillow around with me to provide extra cushioning when I sat down. I also had to wear specially-padded slippers as the cushioning on my heels and the balls of my feet were depleted. My face was gaunt, my hair thin and lifeless, there were bags and shadows under my eyes. My entire body was covered with a fine layer of hair – lanugo – in a feeble attempt to keep me warm. I looked and felt like a walking cadaver, and I frightened the other patients. I even frightened myself, and resorted to covering the mirror in my bathroom with a towel so I wouldn't have to face the creature in the mirror. **> MIRRORS LIE...EVERYONE IS LYING TO YOU...LOOK HOW SKINNY YOU ARE...YOU ARE BEAUTIFUL...THEY ARE ALL JUST JEALOUS <** I was not allowed to leave the ward for the first month, after that I had to be accompanied by a family member. But I felt safe and protected in my 'psych-ward cocoon;' I knew what to expect, my routines consistent and the faces familiar, if not friendly.

An unexpected benefit from my hospitalization was the opportunity to reconnect with a good friend that I had lost contact with. Donna and I met in Grade One and were very good (often best) friends until Grade Ten, when we went to different schools and no longer played baseball together. Donna was always one of the popular girls; she was a kind spirit and I gravitated toward her zest for life. One day a nurse came into my room and asked if I was willing to have a visitor who had called the ward and asked to see me. **> WHO WOULD WANT TO VISIT YOU...THEY JUST FEEL FORCED TO...THEY LAUGH AT YOU...YOU ARE A FAT PIG LOSER AND EVERYONE HATES YOU <** My curiosity was piqued as I thought that I was fully aware of anyone who 'cared enough' to visit me in my self-professed 'prison of shame.' Unbeknownst to me, Donna - who I had not had contact with since the end of high school - was doing a student nursing rotation and had noticed me (in a wheelchair, accompanied by an orderly) in the hospital cafeteria. Due to my drastically declined physical state, she did a 'double take,' doubting her initial recognition of me...*"that's Brenda! No...it can't be her...wait, yes, it is Brenda!"* She struggled with whether or not she should approach me, and decided that it would be most compassionate to let me decide if I was willing to expose my situation to someone new to it. She really was not sure if I would want to see her, so she called the ward and had them pass the message on to me, letting me make the decision. She felt strongly that she wanted to support and love me through whatever was going on in my life. With her love and strength she could help me deal with my shame and others' criticism.

Upon hearing it was my dear (but long-lost) friend, I of course agreed. I put no thought into the fact that I had changed drastically (physically and emotionally) since we had last seen each other and I was craving a friendly face. Often she came to see me after her shift was complete, and we shared some incredibly tough conversations. Donna never judged me, and the bond we shared was very deep. I was able to share with her my darkest thoughts with the knowing that even though she could not understand my specific demon, she truly cared about me. Our close friendship transcended my release from the hospital and my subsequent rollercoaster recovery, and grew deeper over time. Donna had issues in her past, and there were many chats where tears were shed, on both sides of the table. After we both had married and started our families, the busyness of our lives, in separate cities, precipitated another loss of contact. By divine intervention – I now realise that there are no coincidences in life, everything happens for a reason – we have just recently reconnected and I look forward with joy to what this new reconciliation will bring to my life. I remember Donna as an integral part of my recovery, and relied greatly on her constant love and support.

Within a month I had reached the required weight and earned the trust of my doctor to have the privilege of leaving the hospital for the day. However, this much anticipated milestone was a bittersweet experience. I joined my family and relatives to celebrate my youngest brother's birthday. But my reaction to all the people and all the food – mostly all the stares and questions – catapulted me way out of my comfort zone. I ended up returning to my 'safe haven' before my curfew…and in tears.

As the weeks progressed and my weight increased, I found I could concentrate on things other than food, calories and exercise. I took a couple of distance-learning courses that would count toward my third and fourth year university electives. I was beginning to think positively about my future and was proud of my discipline toward these classes.

Finally, eight weeks passed, 17 pounds gained, a million tears shed, and it was time for my discharge. I was finally ready, willing and able to go back home. There were rules to be followed, pacts to be formed, and promises to be made. I was to stick to a diet of 2000 calories/day of the foods of my choice, as long as they covered all the food groups. I was allowed muscle-building exercise only - no cardio. In turn, my family could not make any comments about what or how much I was eating. I was continuing my sessions with Dr. B. – who had actually begun to grow on me and gain my respect – twice weekly but back as an out-patient status. He was still trying to get me on the anti-depressant medication and I was still refusing. He often mentioned that most recovering anorexics go through a phase of bulimia, and perhaps permanently plateau there in their recovery. After all the pain and heartache of dealing with anorexia, there was no way I would allow myself to walk the bulimia path. Underneath his condescending demeanor, however, I do believe he was proud of me.

I discovered a way of thinking of food that assisted me in accepting my weight gain. I would silently bless the food as it entered my mouth, knowing that it was good and loving for me. Blessing the food I needed, instead of cursing it as I previously had, brought me into a different mindset that was essential for my recovery and acceptance of my new way of thinking.

A few days after my return home I flew out to Winnipeg to visit with my university friends. It ended up being an uncomfortable visit; I didn't feel as if I belonged anywhere and everyone was leery of me, not sure how to act. Even JT was cold and distant with me...our attempted reunion was disastrous and further broke both our hearts. I returned home early, feeling unloved and displaced > **WHAT WAS THE**

POINT OF ALL THE EFFORT YOU PUT IN TO YOUR RECOVERY...YOU ARE STILL THE SAME UNLOVED AND PATHETIC CREEP YOU WERE BEFORE...NO-ONE WILL EVER LOVE YOU <

Back home things were getting strained and the celebration of my success was tempered by old recriminations. Dr. B. and I decided I should find full-time work and move out of my parents' house. I transitioned easily into both new situations, returning to my previous summer's employment and moving in with my Aunty Ann. My very best friend throughout my life, my dear cousin Michele, was also living there and we were both excited to spend time together.

My idiosyncrasies followed me wherever I went. One weekend Michele and I decided to spend a couple of days in Banff and stopped in Calgary on our way to pick up our cousin Kim. The three of us spent the day sun tanning and visiting the tourist shops and made plans to go clubbing that night. While Michele and Kim were getting ready to go out, I pulled out my (conveniently) portable 'Rebounder' - a miniature trampoline that I would jump on, wearing wrist and ankle weights - and started exercising. Kim, who was not privy to all my antics, was very blunt and challenged me *"Why the F*** are you exercising? Are you crazy...can't you see how F***ing skinny you are?"* As typical, I ingested and held the hurtful words deep inside of me, yet felt compelled to complete my thirty minutes of 'Rebounding' that I had inwardly committed to. Although we went out and enjoyed ourselves, the evening was peppered with derogatory comments about my weight and *"ridiculous obsession with exercise."*

The job started out great, but it didn't take long to become a nightmare. I was soon labelled as the 'anorexic on ninth' – the office being on the ninth floor of the building - and I often overheard conversations that I shouldn't have; conversations based on my humiliation and the prejudice of my co-workers. I would be invited to join others for lunch and end up being the brunt of their jokes for the rest of the day. One of the ladies I worked with was currently living with a guy that I had briefly dated five years earlier, and acting out of either fear or judgement, she made my life a living hell. I was accused of stealing food from the lunch bags of co-workers **> I WOULDN'T EAT THEIR FATTENING SHIT IF THEY PAID ME <** not knowing how to do my job, and leaving before the end of the work day. All unfounded and all hurtful!

My new living situation also became strained. My aunt got frustrated that I would never eat the food she prepared, and Michele and I bickered often. We shared a room in the basement, and as she was always hot, she required the windows open and the fan on…and I froze. She would snore and I would lay awake all night fuming. I had my idiosyncrasies and silly routines and they drove poor Michele crazy. Her long-time boyfriend and the guy that I was casually dating did not get along. I bought groceries, but only what I would eat. I neglected to lock the door when I was the last one home at night. My living arrangement had become toxic for both Michele and I. I got home one Saturday afternoon and was putting groceries away and Michele told me to *"not bother"* as she wanted me to move out. Of course I took this very personally and felt that yet again I was being cast aside. Everything was always 'all about me,' and I was not able to see the situation from others' perspective. This unbalanced perception negatively affected most of my relationships with important people in my life. I returned to my parents' house with my tail between my legs, my life in shambles. Of course my loving parents welcomed me back with open arms – how easily the pain of the past was forgotten and forgiven. I found it truly comforting to go home to my family after a brutal day at work. I made it through the last month before university classes began broken but not beat.

Going back to university to resume classes was overwhelming and very frightening for me. I was excited to get my life back on track but very concerned with how I would fit in with a new group of classmates. I knew my reputation as an anorexic preceded me, and I would be looked upon with at best scorn, at worst disgust. I found a room to rent off-campus, disregarded my insecurities and approached the friendliest face in my class. I connected with a kind spirit, and was welcomed into her group of friends. I slowly started to feel attractive enough to begin dating again. I was very committed to my education and excelled in my classes. My perfectionism was still alive and well and turned its focus on my studies. My third year of university was my best year on my transcript and after my shameful exit a year earlier, I was so very proud of my academic achievements.

This time frame was not without its anguish though. There were many dark moments when I just wanted to give up and go home. Mom was always able to 'talk me off the ledge' and she became my closest confidante. I was still quite emotionally unstable and relied heavily on her and our telephone conversations. Although I had close friends, I was not comfortable sharing my insecurities with them. I felt I had to portray a strong front...once again, my perspective. I never gave my friends the opportunity to provide me with their support and strength, because deep in my heart I did not trust anyone.

My weight was hovering between 93 and 95 pounds and I was okay with that. I was no longer allowing myself to run, but I did attend a couple of aerobics dance classes each week. My confidence in my social life was growing – I was developing close relationships with a new group of friends and also spending time with some of my previous classmates. The one person I was avoiding was JT, I just wasn't emotionally strong enough to engage in that scenario. We both ended up at the same off-campus party a few times but did not approach each other. I would covertly watch him dancing with other girls, or flirting as they perched confidently on his lap, and my heart would break – just a little more – as I realised what I had lost.

My third year of university progressed smoothly, health-wise, and I ended the year just under 100 pounds. My parents and medical team, headed by Dr. B., were pushing me to break 100 pounds in order that I overcome the mental block of a three-digit weight. They thought I wouldn't be stable until I hit that target. I felt stable, though, and confident that I would not relapse. I was fighting my best fight and vowed never to sink back into the pit of Demon's total control.

My memories of the summer before my last year of university are positive and happy ones. I was dating someone that I had met through my aunt, and we spent every weekend together at the lake waterskiing and having a great time. I had a promising job with a small Interior Design firm and the Principal Designer became my mentor and good friend. Once in a while the blackness returned, but I managed to keep DEMON at bay. My boyfriend, Guy, was understanding and supportive, and encouraged my path toward wellness. His empathy carried me through moments that pulled me back into the role of an anorexic and he truly recognised the efforts I put into my on-going recovery. He never displayed any shame or embarrassment of my weight, whether it was blatant stares from others on the beach, as I was (proudly) displaying my slim physique in a bathing suit, or the concern voiced from his mother regarding *"becoming involved with an anorexic."* Although

I was still very skinny, I appeared as a 'normal skinny,' no longer a deathly corpse. My path to normalcy had begun.

I started my fourth and last year of university at the 99 pound mark. I was proud of how I looked and confident in my recovery – with no episodes of binging – excited to be completing my degree, and in love. Guy and I decided to pursue our relationship long-distance and managed to see each other every six weeks or so. I desperately wanted to start menstruating again, to feel like a complete woman, and really be able to move past the symptoms of my disease. The day I actually had to go out and buy feminine protection I felt like a kid on Christmas morning. I was so excited to be a real woman again!

JT and I were able to renew our <u>friend</u>ship and we spent many enjoyable hours together, getting to know each other on a new level. We now loved each other as friends, and our shared history kept the bond strong in our hearts.

The calendar rolled over to March of 1987 – my thesis was nearing completion and the Graduation Formal was coming up. Great things were on my horizon. Guy was flying out to Winnipeg for the weekend to accompany me to the Grad Formal. My individuality shone through with my fashion statement; rather than wearing a gown for the event, I stood out in the crowd in a 3-piece white tuxedo! However, the weekend was certainly not what I had anticipated…Guy was very distant from the time he arrived, and later that night confessed that he wanted to date other women and felt we should end our relationship. I was devastated, and so confused…why would he agree to be my date for the Grad Formal and fly out to Winnipeg for the weekend, only to break up with me? Foolish or not, we ended up going to the Formal together. I was able to hide my despair from others and ended up having a great time with my classmates. At some point, Guy must've looked at me and realised that he made a mistake in breaking up with me, because he apologised and asked me to forgive him. At the time I was elated and readily agreed, but of course with hindsight, I soon realised I had made a mistake. Less than a month later, as I was wrapping up my time in Winnipeg and readying myself to head back home permanently, Guy called me and broke up with me once again. There was no option of another reunion, and again he broke my heart. I turned to JT for comfort and compassion, and we spent my last evening in Winnipeg together...laughing, crying, sharing memories and contemplating our individual futures. We had no plans to reunite romantically, but our friendship was something to treasure.

Soon classes were officially done, my thesis complete and I packed up my life in Winnipeg for the last time. It was very sad saying my final good-byes to my friends and colleagues, but I carried much pride in the fact that I was alive, that I had completed

my degree, and that I was about to begin a new phase of life. This time I was leaving on my own accord, with my head held high, instead of in shame with my Mom taking me home. DEMON had knocked me down...<u>hard</u>, but I had risen again and was eager to move on.

This...is my triumph (and some tribulations)

My life since then has had many twists and turns and ups and downs, but I can truly say it has been an amazing experience. I never once allowed myself to slip back into the deep pit of anorexia hell. There were many times DEMON tempted me, but I remained strong and others' support and faith in me remained strong. Slowly but surely my weight increased to (the low end of) a healthy range, and my mind was pre-occupied less and less with thoughts of food. My exercise regime was reasonable and kept me toned, slim and firm. Since then I always eat very healthy, and I allow myself the indulgence of my favourites – ice cream, chocolate, and salty snacks - but I am disciplined enough to only need a couple of bites to satisfy my cravings. And I can proudly say I have never had any binge episodes.

Climbing that monstrous, jagged mountain while fighting DEMON the entire journey was the most difficult accomplishment of my life and I hold great pride in it. It took about ten years after my discharge from the hospital to truly sever all the lingering tendrils. I felt people were always watching what and how much I was eating and judging my appearance. For many years I was hurt by others' comments on how 'skinny' I was, and often wondered why people feel they can say hurtful things to a slim person that they would never consider saying to a heavier person. One instance of a tragic hurt that stands out above most others happened during a family gathering at my Grandparent's house. I was well on my road to recovery but still quite slim. My aunt commented on how 'skinny' I was and mentioned to her husband – my Mom's brother – how she wished she was tiny like me. My uncle bellowed out for all to hear that if he *"wanted a broom, (he) would go out and buy one."* That caustic comment stayed with me until his dying day, and so impacted my relationship with him that I (unlovingly) refused to attend his funeral. He may have meant this as a joke, but I was very sensitive about my weight and took everything much too personally. I was weary of being the focus of negative attention, and despised being singled out.

But now, through my spiritual healing, I understand that everyones' perceptions are theirs alone, and how they judge me has nothing to do with the person I am. I have a choice...I can let others' perceptions and judgements hurt me, or I can live true to the light within me and truly love the person I am, and the vessel that contains my spirit – my physical body. For too long I lived as a reflection of others' judgements and felt separate from all the love that I am entitled to. By feeling I was undeserving, I manifested it in all areas of my life, and pitied myself for never being good enough. Because I felt undeserving of love, I built an imposing wall around my heart, and I let no-one in. I thought this would protect me from being deserted by those I loved; what I did not realise is that it separated me from my birthright – the love and acceptance of others, on all levels of my life.

My eating disorder was only one small manifestation of the way I felt inside – the abandonment of my biological Father, my separateness from my family, my feeling of not deserving love. Yet, I truly know that I conquered my eating disorder demon – through diligence, incredibly hard work, and the love and support of others.

But there have been other forms of DEMON that have prevented me from living my authentic life. This is why it is essential to continue self-discovery until the (former) eating disorder sufferer has recognised and can overcome the true cause of their self-limiting beliefs. Because this lack of self-love, for whatever reason it may exist, will attract the Demons of Depression, Anxiety, Addiction, Anger…the list is as long as the mind can project.

Once again I emphasize that although you the sufferer, or you the sufferer's parent, or you the sufferer's partner has witnessed a healing of the physical body, please do not fall under the misbelief that the 'work' is complete.

"There will come a time when you believe everything
is finished. That will be the beginning."
Louis Armour

Once the body is healed, extend your goal to focus on the spirit. Not the mind, but the spirit – that small spark of light within that will continue to flicker on and off until it becomes a light so bright and consistent that it can truly guide the authentic self. At this point the mind will follow. And the new belief that will be present in the heart of the sufferer will extend outward for all others to witness. And your true healing will be complete.

The relationships with those closest to me have definitely changed since my battle with anorexia. I held such shame for so many years that I could not gather the courage to share my story with others, nor even discuss my dark time with those who peripherally walked that journey with me. I was fearful that my parents and siblings also carried this shame, and in turn, felt greatly disappointed in me. During my recent discussions with them, I was pleasantly surprised by the support and pride they all have in me. By my sharing of my darkest memories and the despair I lived with my entire life, a deeper understanding of this disease grew for them. Answers to many questions that lingered for years came to light. No-one realised the deep-set pain that had plagued me and affected my childhood.

The love I share with my siblings is monumental and though we may be very different in our beliefs and life direction, we respect each other for the unique personalities we bring to our family unit.

The love my Mom and I have for each other is unique because of the bond and love we share for my biological father John. We cling to each other as sole survivors of that era. As a mother myself, I am able to appreciate and understand the 'run back into the fire' kind of love that a mother has for her children. And I now know that her purpose during that time was to support and love me through my dark moments. She was 'in the arena' with me all along...beside me, fighting our demon.

The relationship with my (step) Father, Dave, changed the most since my recovery. As a child, I had little love and respect for him, and saw him as the instrument of most of my despair. It was wrong and unfair, but unfortunately, that was my perspective. And although I regret this and am truly sorry, my immaturity and deep-set pain allowed me no control nor ability to change. The first time I allowed my Dad's *"I love you"* into my heart was during the 'Father/Bride' dance I shared with him at my wedding. Through my spiritual healing I was able to view his life situation from a different perspective, and realise that he always loved me, in the way he knew best. I can now let his love shine in my life and offer me all the blessings a father can offer his daughter. My love and respect for him trumps all earlier distress, and I appreciate his presence in my life profusely.

After my recovery from anorexia was complete, and I was confident that particular DEMON was destroyed, I still battled my other demons that loomed large in my life. The problem was that I felt I had depleted all my energy battling anorexia and had no strength left inside. Yes, I had created an amazing family with a wonderful man, yet I was never happy and always searching for love and acceptance. The Demons of Anger, Depression and Addiction still dominated my life after anorexia. They caused hurt and destruction not only for me, but tragically for all those who touched my life. And because of this, the Demon of Guilt became my replacement for the Demon of Anorexia. I hurt many people that I love and that love me.

What finally saved me was my willingness to discover and believe in a process much different than my conventional attempts at therapy and medication. Although my work with psychologists and therapists, and my years of anti-anxiety/ depression medication eased my pain and helped me through some horrible times, I finally realised that I needed more. Not actually more, but different…these healed my mind and were essential to my recovery, but I needed to go deeper than that. I needed to heal my spirit…and finally, after many years of truly being miserable, my revelation occurred….

Danielle, a casual friend and business acquaintance mentioned her participation in the Hoffman process during a lunch gathering. This resonated in me and remained with me although I wouldn't be ready to commit fully for more than a year. My friendship with Danielle grew deeper, we shared many intimate conversations, and she was my inspiration to begin my journey towards complete healing. From there, my universe has expanded and through my committed vow to truly heal my spirit – which in turn healed my mind – I have realigned my thoughts and perceptions of my reality.

I will not get in to a detailed description of my spiritual journey, for that remains to be a future story to be told. But I will mention the important touch-points because they have been essential to me, and may provide some guidance for you...

Through my work with the Hoffman Process, my Life Coach Nik Gardiner - who became an incredible mentor and dear friend, readings of inspirational authors – specifically Marianne Williamson, Dr. Wayne Dyer, Brene Brown and Michael A. Singer, and my study of 'A Course in Miracles', I am well on my way to becoming my authentic self, and living a life I am entitled to.

At age twenty-six I married a wonderful man. Doug was aware of my unhealthy past but did not know me during my dark battle. He was proud of how I looked, and I felt like his Queen walking into a room with him. He supported my food choices, he reassured my Mom when she worried I was slipping back, and he loved me through my bouts of anxiety, depression and self-doubt. But most important, he has honoured my decision to hide my past from those who didn't witness it. It has taken me thirty years to shed my cloak of shame. For indeed, back then mental illnesses were a shameful thing, no-one spoke of them, and few admitted they suffered. I am grateful for the light that is now focused on mental illness in general, and eating disorders in specific. My spirit is finally healed and I am proud that I am able to stand strong and share my story with others.

Doug and I were blessed with four healthy babies – four miracles which I was told I would never have. It is truly amazing that a body which was starved nearly to death was given a new lease on life and was able to conceive, nourish and give birth successfully not once <u>by chance,</u> but four times <u>by choice.</u> My first pregnancy was definitely the toughest mentally, as I was still emotionally healing from the disease, and

gaining pounds and girth was difficult at times. Knowing that I was growing a miracle baby inside me however, enabled me to accept my body's changes. My focus and fear was all about after the baby was born and whether or not I would be able to lose all the 'baby weight.' I am ashamed to say that my initial reason for choosing to breast-feed was not the benefits for the baby, but the help it would give to my ability to lose weight. The joke was on me, however, as I ended up holding on to the last ten pounds until after I stopped breast-feeding, when the rest of the weight and an additional five pounds fell off quickly.

And...breast-feeding quickly became a treasured time for me which I chose to indulge in for about a year with each of my babies. For the record, I gained a healthy amount of weight, within the recommended range of 20 – 35 pounds, with each of my four pregnancies. My children are all healthy, happy, kind and successful. Neither they, nor I, have any health issues due to my anorexia. For this I am truly grateful. At any moment along my journey things could have taken a turn and my life permanently altered, or most likely ended.

I bless my parents, I bless my family, and I bless all those who supported and loved me through my struggles. I bless those who are able to hear my story and choose to understand rather than condemn.

And I bless those who are currently struggling with this tragic disease. May you find the self-love and strength to fight your demon. There is hope, and you will succeed. I stand before you as an example of that hope, just as your family walks beside you, and your angels embrace you.

You are worth it, you are precious...you are loved, loving and loveable!

This... is what I know now

"Eating disorders are real, complex, and devastating conditions that can have serious consequences for health, productivity and relationships. They are not a fad, phase nor lifestyle choice. Eating disorders are serious, potentially life-threatening conditions that affect a person's emotional and physical health. People struggling with an eating disorder need to seek professional help. The earlier a person with an eating disorder seeks treatment, the greater the likelihood of physical and emotional recovery."

[https://www.nationaleatingdisorders.org/get-facts-eating-disorders]

The role of supportive and empowering parents was critical in my recovery process. Attempts at honest, courageous conversations between my parents and myself helped create possibilities for change and recovery. Open communication and mutual expressions of feelings were vital keys to overcoming my disease. This honest communication is imperative right from the start, when the first signs of disturbed behavior are evident. Both the parent and the sufferer may find it difficult to initiate this talk early, when the disease is not openly apparent. Even with a lack of evidence or information on eating disorders, a hug, smile or encouraging word can help to open up the path of communication between the parent and the sufferer. As a parent, it is imperative to trust your intuition. It is better to overreact than to miss an important cry for help. Many initial signs of an eating disorder are behavioral – a decrease in social interaction, secrecy and deception, irritability, excessive exercise, a sudden drop in school grades. Watch your child, <u>hear</u> what they are saying, <u>see</u> what they are doing!

There are usually multiple triggers and factors that contribute to an eating disorder, not one single cause. Every person's story is different, and it is imperative not to treat the sufferer as a 'case study' or try to pigeon-hole into a classic example. Realize that everyone has their own perspective, what you may see as the issue may be very different than how the sufferer views it. Live in the present moment, understanding that each day brings a new chance for hope and recovery.

"Knowingness is not enough, we must apply.
Willingness is not enough, we must do…"
Johann Wolfgang van Goethe

Anorexics and their families often tend to avoid conflict and have high expectations for perfection. Silence breeds anxiety, and stress can create changes in eating behaviors. Food is often used as an outlet of perceived or actual pressure. An eating disorder is a misuse of food to resolve emotional issues. What may start out as a few skipped meals can quickly progress into a purposeful and consistent behavior, with no sense of control. The dichotomy occurs because the sufferer strives for control over her environment and feels that she has the ultimate control of her eating choices. However, the control is only in the hands of the disease.

Being a sensitive individual is often a challenge in which a gift can also become a burden. Noticing feelings in others as well as oneself can bring about caring behavior and self-awareness. However, sensitivity can often provide a breeding ground for eating disorders when one takes the opinions of others too personally. Controlling food can temporarily numb pain from hurt feelings and harsh judgement. As exemplified with my decline, low self-esteem, perfectionism and a sensitive demeanor are typically prevalent in those who develop anorexia. Those who are particularly sensitive need more reassurance and validation than other people, as they tend to be much harder on themselves. Because of my tendency toward perfectionism, I was much more susceptible to becoming obsessive with my weight. Shifting the focus from areas in my life that were unmanageable to the pursuit of thinness was my consistent mind-set. As my disease progressed, my mind became more and more pre-occupied with thoughts of food, drowning out everything else. My deeper issues were suppressed, losing their continued emphasis in my life. I was soon unable to address or even recognize these deeply entrenched problems that led to my life of despair, and eventually the eating disorder.

For me, like most anorexics, exercise became as addictive as food restricting. Rigorous exercise released chemicals in my brain which resulted in a temporary 'exercise high'. However, to continue achieving this feeling, I had to work out more frequently and intensely, extending the length of each work-out. The thought of missing a work-out sent me into an emotional tailspin. My increased anxiety and dramatic mood swings were definite signs that I was spiraling out of control.

A common feeling of those close to the sufferer is the need to 'tread lightly.' My parents, siblings, friends and boyfriend were conscious of my erratic moods and were afraid of saying or doing anything that would 'set me off.' The strain of 'walking on eggshells' around me demanded great restraint and an over-zealous awareness on their part. There was a constant tension surrounding me and no-one felt comfortable letting their guard down and just being themself. I was aware of this tension but blamed others for not understanding what I was going through. Seeing only through the skewed perspective of my demon-driven despair, never once did I accept any responsibility for the negative currents surrounding me.

I was able to satisfy all cravings that may have arisen in the most unusual ways – by calling on all my senses other than that of taste. I often deeply inhaled the delicious smell of neighbours' barbeques along my evening run, convincing myself that the smell of a barbequed steak was enough for me. It was common for me to treat Sanny to a Dairy Queen ice cream cone, sitting across the table watching her and vicariously enjoying the taste through my eyes instead of my mouth. I would hide around the corner of the kitchen, listening with delight to the sounds of the oil spitting in the deep-fryer that Mom was using to make French fries for supper. And when no-one was looking, I would pick up a piece of dessert – a brownie or Nanaimo square – and roll it around in my hands before wrapping it in a tissue and hiding it at the bottom of the kitchen garbage. These, and many more, were my odd rituals for calorie-free enjoyment.

The influence of media, both television and print, was often behind my obsession with thinness and my desire for the 'perfect body.' I thought that in order to be successful, happy, and most importantly loved, I had to be the thinnest. Yet I was not seeing realistically. My perception of the models in the magazines and on the television was grotesquely skewed. It did not matter that I was much skinnier than those I strived to emulate...I still viewed myself as ungainly, fat and ugly.

I always felt that others' needs, wants and feelings were more important than my own. Playing the 'caretaker' role allowed me to focus on others and thereby disconnect with my own needs. This provided fertile ground for my eating disorder as I shut down others who tried to nurture me. During the last couple months prior to my hospitalization, I outwardly manifested my food obsession by insisting that I prepare the evening meal for my family. However, these were not meals that appealed to others as they were all low-calorie and bland. My parents were reluctant to enjoy them, as they did not want to encourage my preferred meal choices nor did they want to instill calorie-consciousness in my young and impressionable siblings. My warped perspective was that nothing I did was good enough for them, and I was a failure in my efforts to nurture others.

No family is immune to eating disorders and anorexia is definitely <u>not</u> a 'first world problem' nor a 'disease of affluence.' This illness attacks every race and every socio-economic level.

It is true that a lack of communication and family togetherness can contribute to the development of an eating disorder, however I grew up in a close-knit family. It was I myself who built the walls around my heart for protection, and held everyone at bay – because I never felt like I belonged... <u>anywhere</u>! I became an empty shell of my former self. I now know that I can only give others what I have an abundance of...only when I am full of self-love am I able to extend this love to others.

Major life transitions can be traumatic, and may tip the scales towards disordered eating. A move to a new school, starting university, divorce or a death in the family can precipitate a loss of the familiar, which can in turn lead to a decline of self-love and connection. I believe that the disconnect from my family and the full responsibility for my well-being when I left for university, along with the need for autonomy in a large group setting, stirred the embers of my deep-set self-hatred and insecurities of my past. My sense of perfectionism urged me to strive for the role of 'most successful dieter.'

Early detection of the disease was concealed by my distance from my family and my refusal to acknowledge the increasingly evident signs. Frequent excuses not to eat with my family, self-imposed isolation from friends, and my choice to wear layered clothing were early signs that my mental psyche was compromised.

When it no longer became possible to hide my issues with food, my parents attempted all they could to intervene. Not only did they encourage and provide psychiatric and medical help for me, they sought counselling for the family, in order that everyone had a communication outlet and a source of age-appropriate information. I don't know if my parents ever blamed themselves; I do know that no-one could force my recovery until I was ready to release my control. The most helpful message my parents gave me was their confidence that I would take the necessary steps toward recovery, and that they supported and loved me every step of the way. My parents were correct in not attempting to be my therapist and 'fix' me on their own, rather they chose to involve professionals to guide me. Although the majority of my decline occurred while I was away at university, when my family was close they attempted to be honest with their every word and action. I may not have appreciated the smile, the loving hug, the listening ear at the time, but when I was ready to release my demon, the importance of these small gestures of love and support were very apparent, and important, to me.

Through the years I was able to discover the hidden messages that underlined my troublesome symptoms. I believe now that my disease evolved as a cry for help, and became the first step on the road to greater recognition of the person I truly am. Just as a bone healed after a break is stronger than before, I gained resilience though my struggles and recovery, a resilience that strengthened me and increased my appreciation for all my blessings.

> *"What is necessary to change a person is to*
> *change his awareness of himself"*
> *Abraham Maslow*

Like many things in life, too much research and reliance on text-book knowledge of anorexia can be detrimental to the individual experience with the sufferer becoming a stereotype. It is important to remember that the sufferer has their own unique story which must be honored to encourage recovery. My recovery was a lonely and frightening journey. Often the deep-rooted problems that I attempted to cover up with my weight obsession reappeared throughout my recovery. I felt even more depressed facing these issues than I did when I attempted to disguise them.

Throughout my story I referred to the disease as 'DEMON', giving it an entity separate from myself. I was not able to view my disease as separate during my suffering and recovery process…it was simply who I was and I allowed myself and others to define me by my disease. Only after many years was I able to sever myself from the destructive and dependent relationship by dealing with emotions and situations I thought insurmountable. I replaced my pre-occupation with weight and exercising with new coping skills. I have realized how much more important I am on the inside than on the outside. Life took on a new exciting texture as I moved beyond my obsession with my appearance and began to focus on making a difference in my world and the world of those closest to me. I began to see myself not as an unloved, unwanted misfit, but as a complex and wonderful person with dreams for the future, and contributions I could offer to others with my own unique gifts.

For a very long time I have searched for my purpose in life. Why was I so severely affected by anorexia and why was I blessed to have fully recovered? Other than my four amazing children, why did *I* survive? It finally became clear...*I am meant to share my story with others who are touched by this disease.* By sharing my journey, I can be the example of hope that remains elusive.

And if I am able to save even <u>one</u> person, it will be worth every step taken. There and back...

"The purpose of life is to discover your gift. The meaning of life is giving your gift away"
David Viscott

I now truly love my body and have a healthy relationship with food. I am no longer segmented in tiny fragments of pain and suffering, but am whole – a unique and precious person saluting my future with courage and determination.

This...is a profound message

"With love and patience, nothing is impossible"
Daisaku Ikeda

...from the Mother:
"If you suspect that your child may be suffering from an eating disorder, seek professional help immediately! And pray..."

...from the Father:
"Try to be stable and supportive, not erratic. Be as available and loving as your child will allow. Don't get discouraged..."

...from the Brother:
"Support and love your sibling through the tough times. Be aware of the seriousness of this disease..."

...from the Sister:
"Be strong. With love, it is possible to deal with whatever life throws at you. Love and support your sibling, with no limits..."

...from the other Brother:
"Treasure all the moments you have together because life is short, and we have no knowledge of how or when things will change..."

...from the Boyfriend:

"Have the confidence and courage to ask the tough questions. Reach out to others for support, don't try to do it all on your own. Be compassionate and recognise that an eating disorder is a mental illness...

...from the Sufferer:

"You are NOT the disease. Open yourself up to the love and support from family and friends. They love you and need you in their life. You are a precious gift to all whose lives you touch – especially your own..."

This...is my *Mom*

Brenda's experience with anorexia was very traumatic for me, and I feared throughout her life that she would die young. Her biological father John, had tragically lost his life at age twenty-four when we were married only thirteen months. He was an only child who lost his mother when he was thirteen years old; she was thirty-seven. After John's untimely death I was afraid Brenda would continue in this pattern and die at a very young age. This was a constant fear for me (especially once she developed anorexia) and my prayers always included my plea "please don't take Brenda from me."

Brenda was always a perfectionist and did well in all areas of her life – school, music, dancing (ballet) and sports. She was always a very caring and responsible child. As her mother, I made it a priority to be involved in her life and felt we had a close relationship. However, I could only be aware of what she chose to share with me and it breaks my heart to have recently learnt of her struggles through life. I did not know that she felt that she was not an important part of our family and that she never felt like she truly belonged. She was, and is...and we all love her so much.

When Brenda was in the dark depths of the disease there were many times when I felt helpless and frustrated. I did not feel confident when she was under the care of Dr. L. – Brenda didn't respect him and I felt like he had dropped the ball with her treatment. Dr. L. and his family attend the same church as we do, and when I see him at mass, many negative memories still surface. Once she was under the care of Dr. B., I felt a bit of the weight was taken off of my shoulders as he seemed much more knowledgeable of eating disorders and was committed to her recovery, no matter how long it may take.

I knew nothing of anorexia until Brenda's fight with it began. I think Dr. B.'s explanations were fairly clear but it was still a waiting game to see how things would really turn out. There were times when I felt we finally had the disease under control, but then she would regress back to square one. I was concerned about the effect on my other three children – not because I was worried that they may 'catch the disease', but rather because my time and energy focused on her care and recovery and this took my attention away from them. I was grateful that despite their young ages, they never complained, and seemed to understand the severity of her condition. I think that they were very concerned about her health and wanted to see her recover over anything else.

I don't recall sharing our struggles with many other people. Of course my family was aware that she was not well, but no-one knew much about anorexia and could not relate to our daily plight. Although we had a couple of family sessions with Dr. B., I often felt quite isolated day by day, as Dave and I had very different approaches for dealing with what was happening – how our life, centered around Brenda at the time, was crumbling.

I am not sure when I finally felt confident that Brenda would overcome anorexia, it came slowly over time. I continued to watch for signs, both positive and negative, for many many years.

Prayers helped me get through her ups and downs. I had an understanding and loving friend who I was able to share my heartache with; who seemed to have a very strong connection to God. I always felt that Sister Maureen's prayer intentions for Brenda's health went straight from her lips to God's ear, and to this day I am so thankful that He healed her. Prayers were what carried us through this very difficult time and helped us to win the fight.

I love Brenda so much, and I carry such pride in her for overcoming this horrible, horrible disease. It was a tough battle for her, for me, and for those close to us; I am so grateful for her recovery and that I still have her in my life.

Jane Burghardt

This...is my Thank You

It has taken a long time – almost thirty years – for my story to be shared. Not because the writing was difficult; in fact, I was amazed how easily the words flowed, but because it has taken me that long to release my shame. I am grateful to my daughters for listening with empathy, love and acceptance when I finally broke my thirty year silence and shared my tragic story with them one emotional Saturday night. If not for their support, my courage to share with others would never have happened.

The good news is that the public has become much more accepting of mental illness, the dialog more open and honest. But there is still a long way to go.

There are so many people that were integral in my journey of healing, and the telling of my story...

First and foremost, my Mom and Dad, for loving, supporting and believing in me – thank you for your prayers. Thank you for being my pillar of strength.

My sister Sanny, for your life-long unconditional love and acceptance. My brothers Greg and Mike, as well as Sanny – thank you for standing with love in the shadow of my illness...I treasure you all.

JT, for your love and support, and especially your courage with your phone call to my Mom. Thank you for your willingness to relive your pain and confusion thirty years later.

Donna, thank you for showing up in my life whenever I need you most. Our friendship transcends both time and distance; I cherish the fact that we can always pick up where we left off...

Danielle, I am forever indebted to you for introducing me to the Hoffman Process, the first step in my healing process.

Nik, thank you for encouraging me to 'dare greatly' and live my life authentically.

Most importantly my family...

Doug, with much love and heartfelt gratitude, I thank you for your understanding and love throughout the years; and more recently, your support of my spiritual journey.

My amazing children Braden, Lauren, Brianne and Jesse – you are my most precious gifts. My love for you and my pride in the incredible young adults you have become is as vast as the universe. Thank you for your love and respect, through the dark and the light.

You are all so precious to me, and I would not be where I am today without you.
I love you...God bless you all.

About the Author

Discovering the reason for her suffering and recovery from anorexia, Brenda realized her life purpose was to be a symbol of hope for current sufferers and their families. In addition to her professional work, Brenda volunteers for the CMHA in Calgary sharing her story with junior and senior high students, and is actively involved with EDSNA. Brenda currently lives in Calgary, Alberta with her precious family.

Printed in the United States
By Bookmasters

.